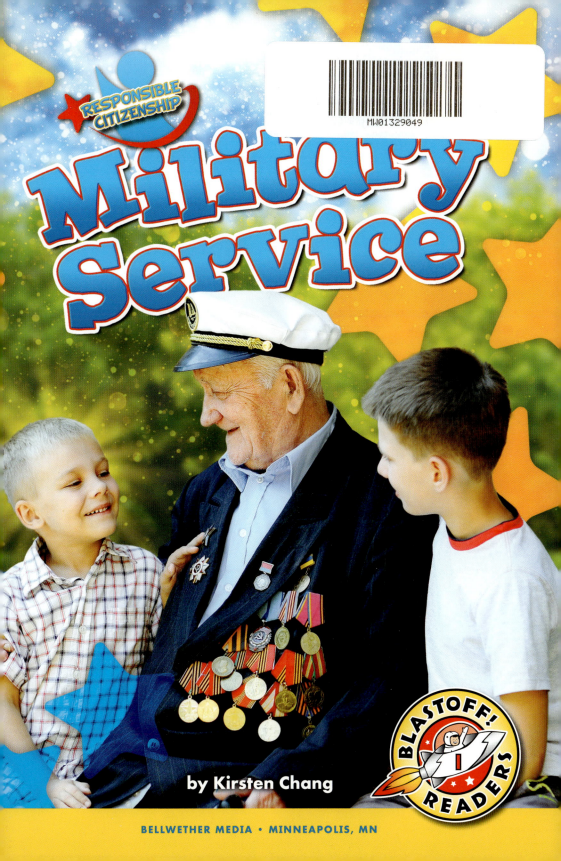

RESPONSIBLE CITIZENSHIP

Military Service

by Kirsten Chang

BLASTOFF! READERS

BELLWETHER MEDIA • MINNEAPOLIS, MN

Blastoff! Readers are carefully developed by literacy experts to build reading stamina and move students toward fluency by combining standards-based content with developmentally appropriate text.

 Level 1 provides the most support through repetition of high-frequency words, light text, predictable sentence patterns, and strong visual support.

 Level 2 offers early readers a bit more challenge through varied sentences, increased text load, and text-supportive special features.

 Level 3 advances early-fluent readers toward fluency through increased text load, less reliance on photos, advancing concepts, longer sentences, and more complex special features.

★ **Blastoff! Universe**

Reading Level

 Grade K  Grades 1–3  Grade 4

This edition first published in 2022 by Bellwether Media, Inc.

No part of this publication may be reproduced in whole or in part without written permission of the publisher. For information regarding permission, write to Bellwether Media, Inc., Attention: Permissions Department, 6012 Blue Circle Drive, Minnetonka, MN 55343.

LC record for Military Service available at http://lccn.loc.gov/2021016562

Text copyright © 2022 by Bellwether Media, Inc. BLASTOFF! READERS and associated logos are trademarks and/or registered trademarks of Bellwether Media, Inc.

Editor: Kieran Downs   Designer: Brittany McIntosh

Printed in the United States of America, North Mankato, MN.

Table of Contents

Serving Your Country	4
What Is Military Service?	6
Why Is Military Service Important?	18
Glossary	22
To Learn More	23
Index	24

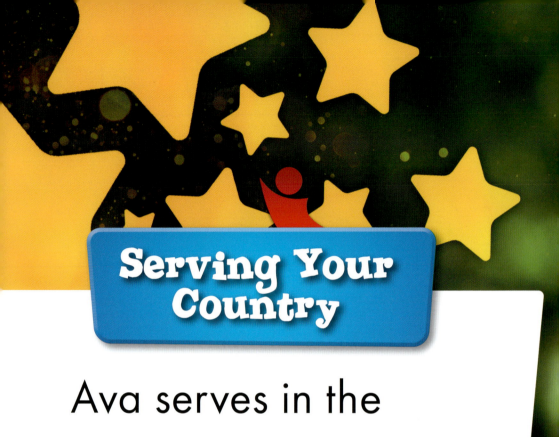

Serving Your Country

Ava serves in the military. She helps keep the country safe.

What Is Military Service?

The military is part of the government. It **defends** the country.

The military helps in **emergencies**. It brings food and health care. It **rescues** people.

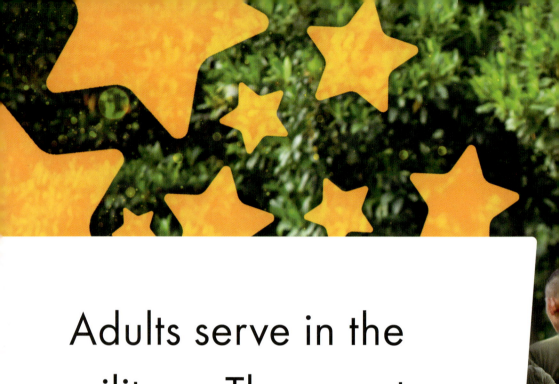

Adults serve in the military. They must be U.S. **citizens**. They must be healthy.

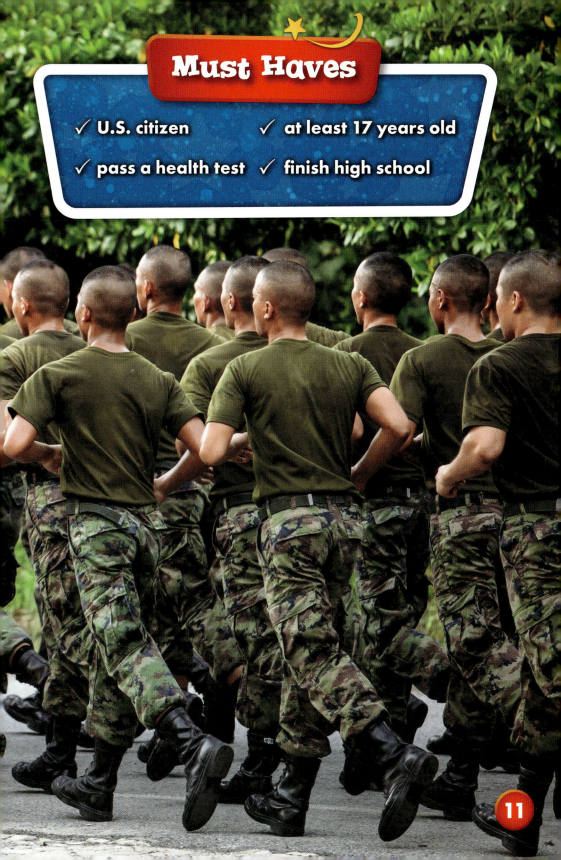

Must Haves

- ✓ U.S. citizen
- ✓ at least 17 years old
- ✓ pass a health test
- ✓ finish high school

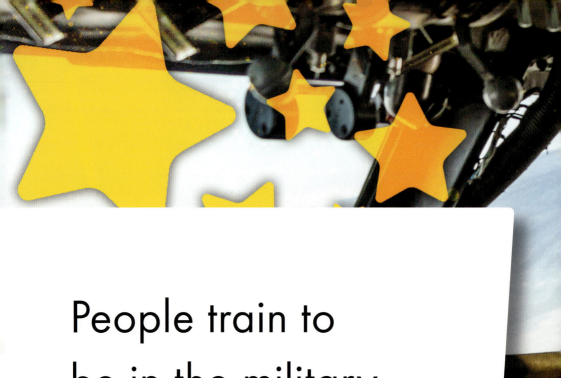

People train to be in the military. Some fly planes. Some sail on ships.

Most members serve for six years. They may join again when their time is up.

Troops often serve in different states or countries.

Why Is Military Service Important?

The military keeps the country safe. It helps in dangerous places.

With/Without

people get help

people may not get help

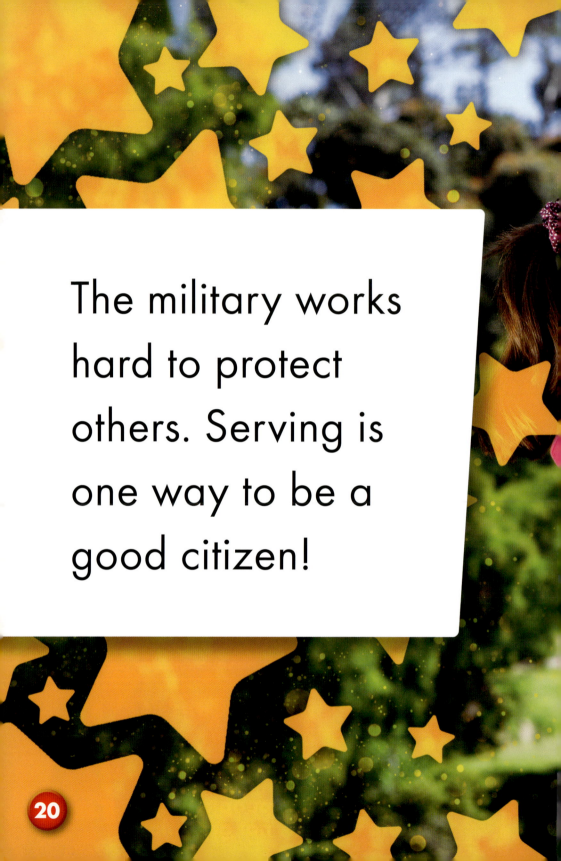

The military works hard to protect others. Serving is one way to be a good citizen!

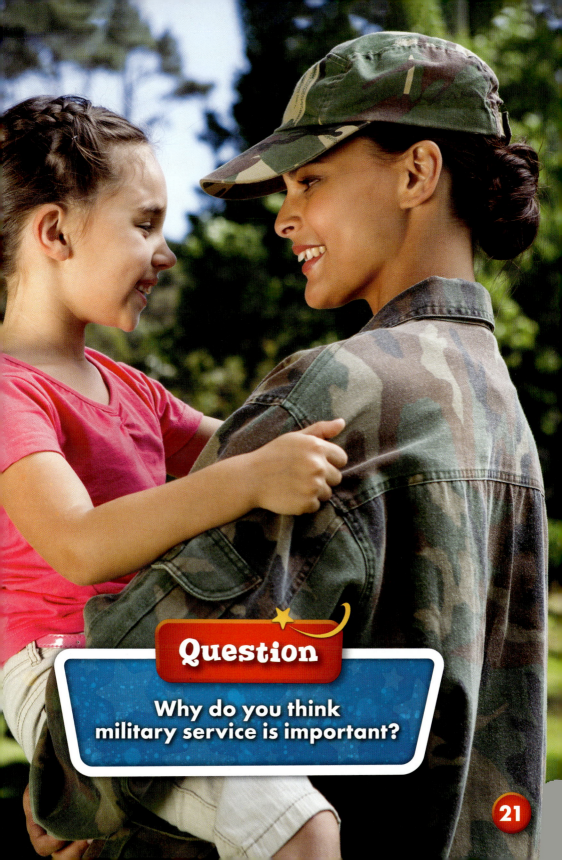

Question

Why do you think military service is important?

Glossary

citizens: people who are members of a certain town, state, or country

rescues: saves people from danger

defends: protects from attacks

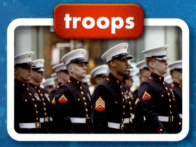

troops: groups of people who serve in the military

emergencies: unexpected situations that need immediate help

To Learn More

AT THE LIBRARY

Alexander, Vincent. *Serving in the Military.* Minneapolis, Minn.: Jump!, 2019.

Reed, Jennifer. *The U.S. Navy.* North Mankato, Minn.: Capstone Press, 2018.

Vonder Brink, Tracy. *The United States Army.* North Mankato, Minn.: Pebble, 2021.

ON THE WEB

FACTSURFER

Factsurfer.com gives you a safe, fun way to find more information.

1. Go to www.factsurfer.com.
2. Enter "military service" into the search box and click 🔍.
3. Select your book cover to see a list of related content.

Index

adults, 10
citizens, 10, 20
country, 4, 6, 16, 18
defends, 6
emergencies, 8
fly, 12
food, 8
government, 6
health care, 8
healthy, 10
helps, 8, 18
must haves, 11
people, 8, 12
planes, 12

protect, 20
question, 21
rescues, 8
safe, 4, 18
sail, 12
serves, 4, 10, 14, 16, 20
ships, 12
states, 16
train, 12
troops, 16
with/without, 19

The images in this book are reproduced through the courtesy of: Evgeniy Kalinovskiy, front cover; DanielBendjy, pp. 4-5; John Moore/ Staff/ Getty Images, pp. 6-7; SOPA Images/ Contributor/ Getty Images, pp. 8-9; Nuk2013, pp. 10-11; guvendemir, pp. 12-13; PR Archive/ Alamy Stock Photo, pp. 14-15; Joe Raedle/ Staff/ Getty Images, pp. 16-17; Gorodenkoff, pp. 18-19; 508 collection/ Alamy Stock Photo, p. 19 (left); Marko Georgiev/ Contributor/ Getty Images, p. 19 (right); wavebreakmedia, pp. 20-21; Rawpixel.com, p. 22 (citizens); Gorodenkoff, p. 22 (defends); FashionStock.com, p. 22 (emergencies); StockPhotosLV, p. 22 (rescues); Stuart Monk, p. 22 (troops).